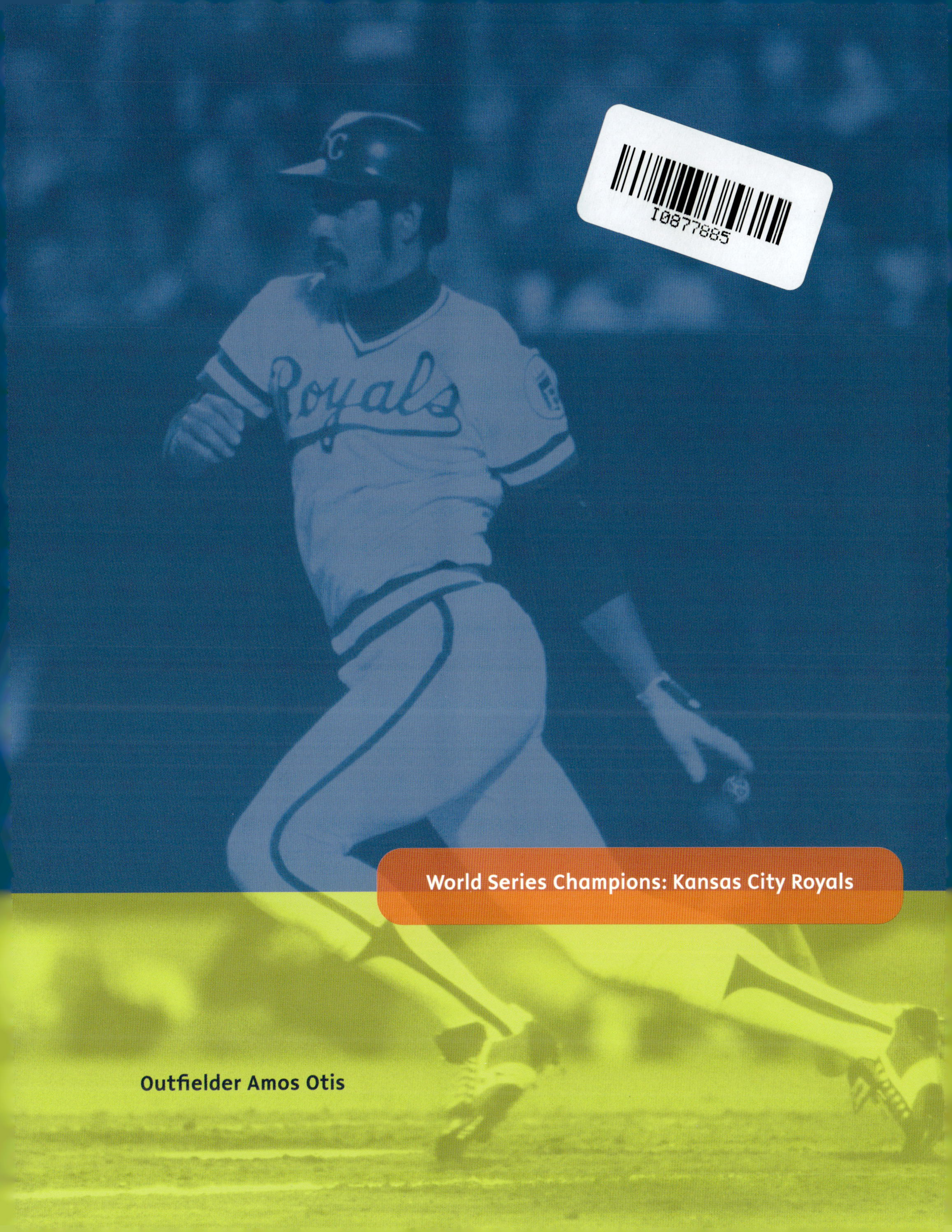

World Series Champions: Kansas City Royals

Outfielder Amos Otis

I0877885

Outfielder Alex Gordon

WORLD SERIES CHAMPIONS

KANSAS CITY ROYALS

JOE TISCHLER

CREATIVE EDUCATION / CREATIVE PAPERBACKS

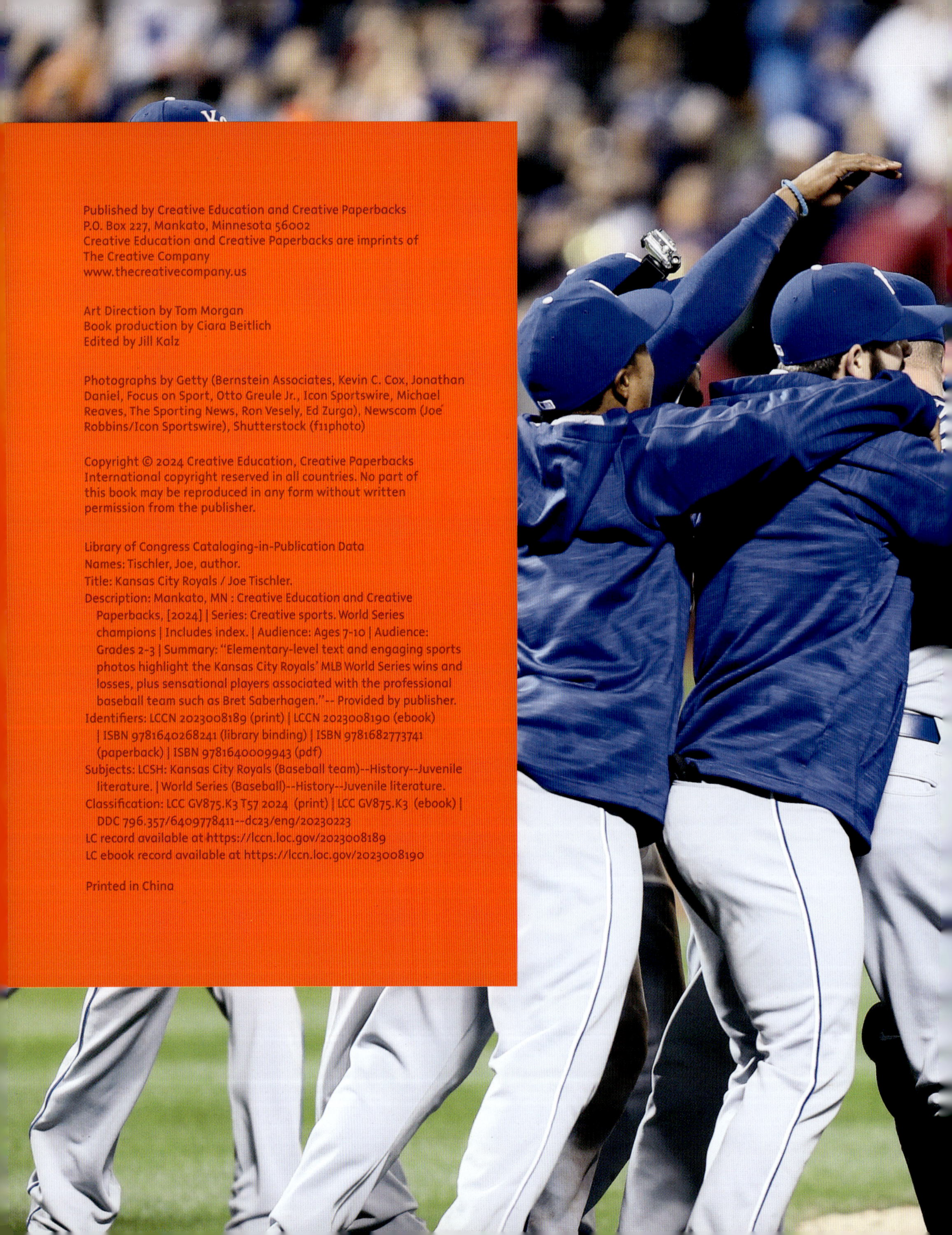

Published by Creative Education and Creative Paperbacks
P.O. Box 227, Mankato, Minnesota 56002
Creative Education and Creative Paperbacks are imprints of
The Creative Company
www.thecreativecompany.us

Art Direction by Tom Morgan
Book production by Ciara Beitlich
Edited by Jill Kalz

Photographs by Getty (Bernstein Associates, Kevin C. Cox, Jonathan Daniel, Focus on Sport, Otto Greule Jr., Icon Sportswire, Michael Reaves, The Sporting News, Ron Vesely, Ed Zurga), Newscom (Joe Robbins/Icon Sportswire), Shutterstock (f11photo)

Copyright © 2024 Creative Education, Creative Paperbacks
International copyright reserved in all countries. No part of this book may be reproduced in any form without written permission from the publisher.

Library of Congress Cataloging-in-Publication Data
Names: Tischler, Joe, author.
Title: Kansas City Royals / Joe Tischler.
Description: Mankato, MN : Creative Education and Creative Paperbacks, [2024] | Series: Creative sports. World Series champions | Includes index. | Audience: Ages 7-10 | Audience: Grades 2-3 | Summary: "Elementary-level text and engaging sports photos highlight the Kansas City Royals' MLB World Series wins and losses, plus sensational players associated with the professional baseball team such as Bret Saberhagen."-- Provided by publisher.
Identifiers: LCCN 2023008189 (print) | LCCN 2023008190 (ebook) | ISBN 9781640268241 (library binding) | ISBN 9781682773741 (paperback) | ISBN 9781640009943 (pdf)
Subjects: LCSH: Kansas City Royals (Baseball team)--History--Juvenile literature. | World Series (Baseball)--History--Juvenile literature.
Classification: LCC GV875.K3 T57 2024 (print) | LCC GV875.K3 (ebook) | DDC 796.357/6409778411--dc23/eng/20230223
LC record available at https://lccn.loc.gov/2023008189
LC ebook record available at https://lccn.loc.gov/2023008190

Printed in China

2015 World Series Champions

Outfielder Willie Wilson

CONTENTS

Home of the Royals

The city of Kansas City, Missouri, is well known for its barbecued food and its water fountains. You can find both of them at Kauffman **Stadium**. The Royals baseball team plays there. Fans love to see them hit home runs over the fountains.

The Kansas City Royals are a Major League Baseball (MLB) team. They play in the American League (AL) Central Division. Their **rivals** are the Chicago White Sox and the St. Louis Cardinals. All MLB teams try to win the World Series to become champions.

Outfielder Carlos Beltrán

Naming the Royals

The team's name has nothing to do with kings and queens. Kansas City has a long history with **livestock**. Every year, the American Royal Livestock Show is held in the city. The name "Royals" was picked from a fan contest based on this event. The team logo still uses a crown. A crown is associated with royalty.

Third baseman George Brett

Royals History

The Royals started play in 1969. They had success early on. They won their first division **title** in 1976. An early star was third baseman George Brett. He played in 13 straight All-Star games. Brett was named the AL Most Valuable Player (MVP) in 1980.

Second baseman Frank White was a great fielder. He won eight Gold Glove Awards. The best fielders at each position get this honor.

Kansas City played in two World Series in the 1980s. They lost to the Philadelphia Phillies in 1980. They won their first World Series title in 1985! In an all-Missouri series, they beat the St. Louis Cardinals in seven games. Pitcher Bret Saberhagen threw a **shutout** in Game 7. He was named World Series MVP.

Pitcher Bret Saberhagen

Outfielder Bo Jackson

The Royals didn't return to the World Series for nearly 30 years. In 2014, they fell to the San Francisco Giants in seven games. They went back to the series the next year. The Royals beat the New York Mets. They were champions again!

Other Royals Stars

The Royals have had many stars. Amos Otis and Willie Wilson formed a strong outfield combination. They each appeared in multiple All-Star games.

Righthanders Kevin Appier and Zack Greinke were two of the best pitchers in team history. Greinke won a Cy Young Award. It goes to the league's best pitcher.

Pitcher Zack Greinke

Catcher Salvador Perez

Mike Sweeney was one of the league's best hitters in the 2000s. He made five All-Star games. Outfielder Alex Gordon won eight Gold Gloves. Salvador Perez is one of the best catchers in baseball. He excels with his bat and his glove. Royals fans hope their team can bring another title to Kauffman Stadium soon.

About the Royals

Started playing: 1969

League/division: American League, Central Division

Team colors: blue, gold, and white

Home stadium: Kauffman Stadium

WORLD SERIES CHAMPIONSHIPS:

1985, 4 games to 3 over St. Louis Cardinals

2015, 4 games to 1 over New York Mets

Kansas City Royals website: www.mlb.com/royals

Glossary

livestock—animals raised for use and profit, such as cattle and pigs

rival—a team that plays extra hard against another team

shutout—a game where one team doesn't score

stadium—a building with tiers of seats for spectators

title—another word for championship

First baseman Mike Sweeney

Index